The
Xenophobe's Guide to
The Italians

Martin Solly

RAVETTE BOOKS

Published by Ravette Publishing Ltd.
P.O. Box 296
Horsham
West Sussex RH13 8FH
Telephone: (01403) 711443

Editor – Catriona Tulloch Scott
Series Editor – Anne Tauté

Cover design – Jim Wire
Printer – Cox & Wyman Ltd.
Production – Oval Projects Ltd.

An **Oval Project**
for Ravette Books.

Acknowledgement and grateful
thanks are given to Federico Tibone
for his help and information.

Contents

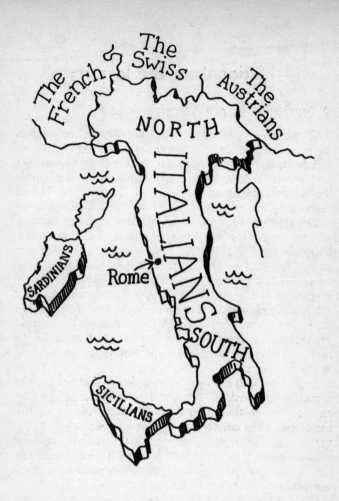

The Italian population is 57 million (compared with 7 million Swiss, 7¾ million Austrians, 10 million Greeks, 48 million English; 57 million French, 80 million Germans, and 256 million Americans).

Italy is 7 times larger than Denmark and 3 times larger than Austria, but could fit into France nearly twice.

Nationalism and Identity

A Nation Without Identity

The Italians are not a race, but a collection of peoples. They tend to think of themselves and each other first and foremost as Romans, Milanese, Sicilians or Florentines, and secondly as Italians. There is little that really links Turin and Bari, or Naples and Trieste, except the autostrada, the rail network and the Catholic Church.

The regions of Italy are very different from one another, and the deeply-ingrained regionalism is quite understandable, considering that Italy has only existed as a nation since 1861, before which the Italian peninsula consisted of several independent states. The unification process required a skilful exercise in geopolitical patchwork, and the leading politicians of the time were well aware of the difficulties ahead. Cavour, who masterminded the process, said: "Italy has been made at last; now let us make the Italians." Were he alive today, he would still be working at it.

Every now and then the Italians do try and behave like a nation and make a big effort to be nationalistic, for example, when the Italian football team is doing well in the World Cup, or Alberto Tomba has just won ten skiing trophies in a row. But mostly the Italians feel like Italians when they are expatriates: in an ice-cream parlour in Melbourne, down a Belgian mineshaft, or at a soccer match in the United States.

On the positive side, the absence of strong nationalistic feelings makes Italians wary of warmongering and jingoism. Knowing that most disputes can be resolved by a mixture of compromise, appeasement and bribes, Italians will do their best to avoid confrontation. In fact, any foreign power planning to invade Italy should consider making an offer before wasting soldiers' lives. If the price is right, it is quite conceivable that the Italians might just agree to sell their country.

Campanilismo

Identity is important to the Italians. Perhaps because they are slightly uncertain about their 'Italian-ness' and not exactly sure what their national identity actually entails, they are particularly attached to their roots. "Where do you come from?" is an important question for Italians which requires a good answer. Unlike the Englishman or American, no Italian is ever at a loss when asked this question. He does not stutter, "I'm not really sure. Let me think for a moment. I live in London, but I was born in Hertfordshire, but then my parents moved to Leeds, and I went to university in Bristol and then my first job was in Southampton..."

Italians know exactly where they come from, and will carry that place around with them for life, like a standard. The man from San Giorgio in Puglia who lives in Turin will always refer to himself and be referred to as *il Pugliese*. He will behave and be expected to behave in a different way from the Torinese. His links with San Giorgio will be maintained all through his life. Even if he left the town thirty years ago, and only goes back once a year to see his second cousins, he will still have to help anyone else who comes from San Giorgio. Similarly, successful tycoons and politicians are supposed to look after their hometowns, investing money in them and finding work for their fellow townsfolk.

Stating where you come from is closely linked to the key Italian concept of *campanilismo*, which literally means 'loyalty to your local bell-tower', but really involves thinking that your village or town is the best in the world. Italians have always loved their hometowns and found it hard to be exiled from them.

This civic pride, however, also implies great competition, and this is especially strong between neighbouring villages, towns, provinces and regions. The rivalry is often so fierce that Italians have little time left for much else, for they know that other human beings, and especially Italians from other families, villages, towns or regions, are sadly lacking in self-discipline, and cannot be trusted. How wonderful Italy would be without *gli altri* – 'those other' Italians.

How Others See Them

The typical stereotype of the Italians is that of a noisy, passionate, scheming, Mediterranean people, whose brilliance and inventiveness is unfortunately marred by laziness and unreliability. Italians are known to live in a beautiful country full of art treasures. They are seen as a happy, fun-loving people, with a genius for design, fashion and food. They are known to be wonderful at singing and at cooking, and terrible at organising and queuing. Italian men have greased-back hair, nine-inch hips and are demon lovers. Italian women are incredibly attractive until they marry, when they immediately become short, fat, overweight mammas.

Italo-Americans often imagine that Italy hasn't changed since their great-grandparents left it at the turn of the century. When they finally come to Italy to find their roots and visit their cousins, they are surprised that not all families are poor, have ten children and live in one room which they share with a donkey and a mongrel, that not all the women wear black and work in the fields, nor do all the men wear hats and sit in bars all day long. They discover that Italy is, in fact, one of the world's most advanced countries, where most families have at least two cars and live in houses that don't just have running water and electricity, but televisions, videos, cellphones and bidets with adjustable jets.

Special Relationships

Because of the massive emigration from Italy at the end of the 19th and beginning of the 20th centuries, there are extensive Italian communities in the United States, Argentina, Uruguay and Australia. There are about 20 million Americans with Italian surnames. But Italo-Americans, Italo-Argentinians and so on are only likely to be regarded as 'Italians', rather than as Americans or Argentinians, if they are rich and successful. So Frank Sinatra, Robert De Niro, Francis Ford Coppola and Sylvester Stallone are all considered to be Italian, and not American. Being embraced so warmly can sometimes have its drawbacks – successful paternity suits are still being brought in the Naples courts against the Italo-Argentinian, Diego Maradona, years after he returned home to Argentina.

How They See Rich Foreigners

Italians love foreigners, especially rich foreigners. The Austrians, Swiss and especially Germans have always enjoyed Italy's climate, culture, beaches and lifestyle. Italy is their playground. Ever since the days of the Roman Empire, Goths have been heading across the Alps to let off steam. The Italians have tolerated them for centuries and are quite happy to go on doing so, as long as the six million who now come to Italy every year spend lots of money and return north again.

The French are considered arrogant and disproportionately proud of themselves. They are seen to look down on their transalpine neighbours, which peeves the Italians no end. But the really unforgivable French sin is to have captured the world market with their inferior wine, which no sane Italian would buy.

The relationship between the English and the Italians is more complex and perhaps more an attraction of opposites. The English like the violent smells, noises, colours, passions and chaos of Italy, while the Italians are fascinated by the calm and order of the English.

Italians know that everything works much better abroad. But they also know that, in real terms, foreigners are less well-off than they are, because they don't live in a beautiful country with plentiful sunshine, they dress badly, and they eat and drink badly, all of which perhaps explains why foreigners have always had their eye on Italy, and taken an interest in the *bel paese*, perhaps too much of an interest.

A surfeit of foreign invaders (Germans, French, Spanish, Austrians, Normans, Arabs), many of whom the Italians had to spend a lot of time (even centuries) getting rid of, has given Italians an inbuilt wariness of foreign domination. This was only tolerated if the Italians got something in exchange. A well-known saying in Roman dialect runs: *Franza o Spagna, purché se magna* ('France or Spain, it doesn't matter, as long as we have something to eat').

Being a curious people, the Italians are fascinated by

9

foreigners and their barbaric ways of life and customs. They love reading and hearing about other nations and going abroad on holiday as this serves to confirm what they already know, that they come from the best place in the world, certainly in terms of the important things in life like sunshine, drink, food and football.

Deep down, the Italians believe that, although other countries might be more powerful and better organised than Italy, in reality the rest of the world behaves the same way they do and is just as corrupt as they are, only sometimes the others are smarter at not being caught.

How They See Poor Foreigners

Foreign immigration is a comparatively recent phenomenon in Italy. Traditionally, the word 'immigrant' has been used by Italians for Italians from other parts of Italy who have moved to their area. But since the late 1980s more and more people have made their homes in Italy, especially from Albania, Eastern Europe, Senegal and the Maghreb countries.

The Italian attitude towards the peoples of southern Europe and northern Africa is a mixture of solidarity and disdain. They like their colour and are fascinated by their strange habits, and they especially like the fact that the immigrants do work that they might otherwise have to do. They agree with the sentiment expressed in the Oscar-winning Italian film *Mediterraneo,* that all the people around this sea compose *una faccia, una razza* (one face, one race). Yet they resist being associated with poor immigrants, like the Albanians or North Africans who offer to clean the windows of their car at traffic lights, for fear that their glamorous image might get tarnished.

How They See Themselves

The Italians see themselves as passionate and charming and they like to act the part for the benefit of foreigners.

They know they are privileged, living in Italy, but they fight hard to keep at bay a nagging feeling of being the Cinderella of Europe. The reluctance of certain nations to embrace the European Union is bewildering for the Italians, who would be more than happy to contract out the running of their country to Brussels.

With unwitting masochism, Italians genuinely rather enjoy seeing their faults thrown back at them. It confirms their own deep-rooted feeling that *gli altri Italiani* are not quite up to the western world's high standards of reliability.

But no criticism is ever taken seriously enough to attempt remedial action. Italians regard it as unnecessary to change their ways, partly because they fear it would be a lost cause, and partly because it suffices periodically to devalue the lira to keep tourists flocking to the *bel paese* with bulging wallets. In any case, foreigners seem to find the locals agreeable and entertaining, or at least tolerable, so it cannot be all bad.

North and South

The Italians often simplify their internal differences by means of a straightforward North-South divide.

The Northern Italian views the Southerner as a corrupt, half-Arab peasant who tolerates the mafia and lives off the income generated by the hard-working North. The Southern Italian views the Northerner as a semi-literate, half-Austrian or half-French unwashed peasant who, by accident of birth, dwells in the richest part of the country

11

and lives off the income generated by the Southerners who work for him in his factories or on his land.

While both these pictures are exaggerated, enough Italians believe in them for the Northern League (a political party promoting a federalism that is not far from separatism) to be a serious force in Italian politics.

The difference in diet, habits and language between the two areas is sufficient to continually fuel these views. The Southern Italian diet is based on pasta and olive oil, the Northern Italian diet on maize, rice and butter. And the language variations are so great that in 1995 *L'amore Molesto*, an Italian film made in the South of Italy, was actually dubbed for the North Italian market.

There is a real danger of Northerners blaming everything they think is wrong in Italy, or that they don't like in the Italian character, on Southerners. So, for example, they see the corruption that riddles Italian politics and government as a 'southern disease', carefully ignoring the fact that the heart of Italy's latest and greatest corruption and graft scandal, *tangentopoli*, was the great northern Italian city of Milan.

The extremists of the Northern League and the Southerners who drive around in cars with the Confederate flag on them only exacerbate the problem: both conveniently forget that if all the Southerners went home, South Italy would be without the economic support of the Northerners, and North Italy would be without hairdressers.

Forewarned

Italy is a country of contradictions. It is the country of the Catholic Church, but also of the mafia. It is the most pro-European country in Europe, but one of the worst at implementing EU directives. It has some of the world's most advanced engineering, but some of its most antiquated plumbing. It is a country of enormous wealth and of extreme poverty.

As an American ambassador put it when he was returning home after completing his stint at Rome, "Italy is a very poor country with a lot of very rich people living in it." This opinion appears to be backed by statistics: in 1992, the European Union announced that Lombardy was the richest region in the Union. But Italians like to think that they are poor and that the citizens of all northern European countries are much richer than they are, but are just better at hiding their wealth.

Character

On Stage

The Italians are great actors and their lives often appear to be one big act. Most of Italian life is spent in public, on show, and Italians know the importance of *bella figura* (cutting a fine figure). Whether they are shopping in the supermarket or modelling clothes, working in the office or directing the traffic, serving in a restaurant or going to see the doctor, the Italians know how important it is to act the part, and look the part as well. They learn how to act when they are children and go on acting throughout their lives.

Because ordinary Italian life is lived on stage, Italian theatre often looks as if it is overacted – it has to be, to differentiate it from the high drama of real life.

You Are What You Wear

Italians always take great care to wear the right clothes on the right occasion. This is never a casual choice – it is important to wear the proper clothes for the role you are playing. The station master must look like a station master and wear his uniform. He must act the part properly, too, as he is on stage in the great film set of life. This is where style is so important. The taxi-driver, the teacher, the doctor, the lawyer and the engineer must all dress, act and behave like taxi-drivers, teachers, doctors, lawyers and engineers.

Taking life easy and being seen to take things easy, whether you are at the beach, in the disco or even at work, is part of *bella figura*, which explains why Italians are often happy to work in jobs that might seem very boring, such as lifeguards or security guards. There they can be on show all the time and be seen to be looking good and taking it easy – on the beach, or hanging around the bank looking important dressed up as a gun-slinger. It doesn't matter that the job is not so pleasant in winter, nor whether the guard is actually able or even allowed to use the gun, as long as he looks the part.

Nowhere can this be seen better than in the world of sport. It makes no difference if you can't swim very well, for that sub-aqua course you must have the right clothes and gear and style and you must look and act like a sub-aqua diver. This is why the latest fashion is important, for it makes your performance more convincing. Many Italian lofts are full of sportswear and gear, bought at great expense, but abandoned because they are out of date or their owner has taken up another activity.

Sports are often taken up just for the look. Cross-country skiing enjoyed a boom when skin-tight Lycra ski-suits were invented. It was worth braving the freezing cold and the physical agony of this tiring sport for a couple of hours in order to be able to show off in the bar afterwards (and it might even have been good for your health, too).

Italians are very observant of how other people dress, particularly foreigners who are generally considered to dress badly. During the Second World War the British prisoners of war who managed to escape from prison camps had far more problems travelling in Italy than in any other country in Europe. The suits and clothes they made from their uniforms, sheets and blankets often took in the Germans, but rarely fooled the Italians.

Allegria

Allegria is a general effervescence and delight in living that is not easy for the outsider to penetrate. It is linked to the joy of being and tends to involve sunshine, company and collective high spirits and it is why Italians so often seem to be laughing and smiling together.

Allegria is infectious and not sharing in it is regarded as bad form. All those attending that big family picnic in the mountains will demonstrate *allegria* in a big way, roaring with laughter at Uncle Gianni's imitation of Aunt Rita sitting down on a cactus by mistake, even if they have heard the story countless times before.

The counterpart of *allegria* is a depressing form of melancholy and suffering that visitors are usually spared, since it is often brought on by the damp, cold weather of late autumn and coincides with the seasonal increase in prices and taxes.

But generally speaking, the Italians tend to look on the bright side of life – a positive outlook aptly illustrated by their touching salutation: "May the saddest days of your future be the happiest days of your past."

Status and Success

Italians are not in the least bit snobbish, and their only real social divisions are based on wealth. Those who have money, even temporarily, may spend it and flaunt it where and how they like. They will be treated as potentates – as long as they have enough, of course.

The one thing that captures the imagination of Italian males more than the dream of being a star footballer is *owning* a major football team. As a business, everyone knows it's unprofitable, but as an image-booster, it's the tops. It is not by chance that the Agnelli family (of Fiat fame) are at the helm of Turin's Juventus, and it was not sufficient for the highest flying *arrivista* (parvenu) of his generation, Silvio Berlusconi, to own major media networks; he had to buy A.C. Milan in order to be seen as a real success.

Behaviour

The Art of Getting By

Italians are past masters at *arrangiarsi* (getting by), and at home and in communities abroad have always been famous for their ability to make the best of their situation. This is due to the fact that Italians more often than not have had to, and sometimes still have to, get by in their own country.

For example, when the traffic is held up by two drivers having a long conversation because they haven't seen each other since the day before, those in the traffic queue will make the most of the moment by fiercely sounding their horns and hurling insults, or reading their newspapers, or making phone calls while using the rear-view mirror to preen.

When, through a mixture of governmental incompetence and bureaucratic venality, Italy suffered a shortage of small change in the 1970s, the Italians just shrugged their shoulders and used sweets instead.

Giving Presents

The Italians are generous people, but their generosity should be accepted with caution, for no present in Italy comes without strings attached. Italian life and power is based on a system of gifts and favours. The moment someone accepts a gift, he owes the giver a favour and has concluded an agreement that lasts a lifetime. So when one Italian gives another a lift to the station or the telephone number of a good eye specialist, sooner or later he will expect something back.

Driving

Driving is the area of his life where the Italian male really comes into his own, and he feels he can properly express himself. Ask what he means by a good driver or a beautiful road and he will wax poetic. He will tell you that a good driver is one who drives at speed from A to B, ensuring the maximum pleasure and comfort of his passengers, not braking too often, not driving over bumps or holes but slaloming round them, driving, in short, like a Ferrari Formula One team member. A beautiful road is a wide, well-cambered road, which can be driven at high speed without any unsettling bumps for his passengers, in short, a race track; the narrow, scenic road winding through the mountains will not be considered a beautiful road.

Owners of new Alfa Romeos are recommended by the company's manual to drive in a certain way to get the best performance and life expectancy from their vehicle: they should not drive too close to the car in front, they should not accelerate or brake suddenly between traffic lights; they should not corner at high speed, and so on... In other words they should not drive as Italians.

Country bumpkins who drive in Italian cities need to remember two basic rules: vehicles with out-of-town plates are regarded as fair game by both local drivers and traffic police; and traffic police enforce the traffic laws as and when they wish. It is said that in Naples there are only two kinds of traffic lights: those that are there for decoration and those that are merely a suggestion.

Driving in the countryside can be entertaining, too, particularly when you don't know where you're going. Italian sign painters specialise in artistic roadsigns designed not to help motorists, but to be appreciated as masterpieces of art by those who live nearby. Fortunately it is not easy to get lost in Italy, as long as you already know the way and remember that, despite the efforts of the autostrada administration to convince drivers that they do, not all roads lead to Rome.

Manners and Etiquette

Italians are courteous people, and well-mannered. Greetings are important and, since the Italians are very physical, hand-shaking and kissing are the norm. They convey genuine warmth and pleasure at seeing people again, even if they have seen them the day before or even that morning. Kissing is on both cheeks and there are no taboos about men greeting each other this way. Hand-shaking has the added advantage of revealing that neither party is holding a weapon.

The Italians are enthusiastic and call one another *cara* and *bella* at the drop of a hat. Yet before crossing someone's threshold they will ask "*Permesso?*" (May I have permission?).

Ciao is an informal greeting used both on meeting and on departure. *Buongiorno* (Good day) is used for most of the day until a certain point in the late afternoon, when people will greet each other with *Buonasera* (Good evening), as if the afternoon did not exist. They are much more rigid about the difference between evening and night, and "What did you do last night?" will be regarded as a nosy or even impertinent question, but "What did you do yesterday evening?" won't raise any eyebrows at all.

The Italians have three possible forms of addressing one another: the *tu*, *voi* and *lei* forms. The *tu* form is used in the family, by young people with one another and by adults who know each other well. Today's preferred polite form is *lei* rather than *voi*.

Strangers are addressed as *signor* and *signora*. *Signora* is generally used even if the woman is technically *signorina* (an unmarried one). Professional titles are much more widely used than in Britain and America. *Dottore* is not used just for medical doctors, but for any form of graduate; *professore* is the term for all teachers, not just at university; not only composers, but craftsmen and even judo teachers, are called *maestro*; *ingegnere* is very highly prized, reflecting the high status that engineering graduates enjoy. Professional or honorary titles are also often used for famous people, so Giovanni Agnelli is referred to as *l'avvocato* and Silvio Berlusconi as *il cavaliere*. Nobody minds if the professional titles are not used in exactly the right way, as long as they flatter the recipient.

Grazie and *prego* are the mainstay of Italian manners, but it is not considered rude to ask for a coffee in a bar by saying in a loud voice, "A coffee"; one is buying a service and being over-polite could be considered as false politeness and therefore rude.

Italians are incapable of saying sorry in the English sense; if they are not sorry, they feel they don't need to say anything, and if they are sorry, they can say it in the confessional.

Punctuality

Punctuality is only relatively important in Italy and the time is often treated as approximate. Being late for appointments is tolerated rather than welcomed – a quarter of an hour is acceptable, but half an hour is not. So university professors will turn up for their lectures up to a quarter of an hour after the scheduled start, but if they pass that deadline they will find the lecture theatre empty.

Queuing

The Italians could never be considered good at queuing; in fact, the idea of standing in line tends to make them laugh. The scrummage that occurs while waiting to go on the chairlift at ski resorts, or to buy tickets for a football match or a concert, occasionally creates real problems of a not necessarily good-natured kind.

The introduction of number dispensers in some of the places where the worst fights used to break out, such as public offices and fish counters at the supermarket, is to some extent solving the problem. The Italians enjoy collecting the tickets and like the idea of the implied 'fair play'. But the novelty is already beginning to wear off, and at some of the busier public offices, a new game has begun: getting to the office early and queuing up for tickets, then selling them at an outrageous price to those who arrive late and risk not being served before the office closes.

La Famiglia

The family is far and away the most important social, economic, organisational and political unit in Italy. The family can be nuclear or extended.

The nuclear family is divided into: the father, the head of the family, who thinks he does all the work and decision-making; the mother, who in actual fact does all the hard work and takes all the important decisions; the male children, who are always spoilt and never really learn how to compete efficiently; and the female children, who are never spoilt and as a result are far more capable than their brothers with whom they have to compete at a disadvantage from a very early age.

The extended family is a very large-scale social unit, including all possible relatives. It is seen at christenings, weddings, and funerals, and generally involves large numbers of people. Family functions are occasions of enormous ostentation and generosity, where the pecking order of power and wealth in the family is carefully evaluated. An Italian will even go as far as to pretend to be seriously ill in order not to go to a second cousin's wedding where he fears he might cut a *brutta figura* if he hasn't got enough money for an expensive present and a new suit.

The Italian family is a highly-sophisticated network of patronage and power held together by a complex system of exchanging presents and performing favours.

Going against the wishes of the family is hard and in reality nearly impossible for most Italians. Young Italians rarely leave the nest and, even when they do, it is usually only to move into the house across the road, or the flat next door. Statistics published in 1994 showed that nearly three-quarters of 27 year-old Italians still lived at home.

Il papà

Behind every great Italian man there is a great Italian woman, sometimes his wife or his mistress, but usually his mother. The Italian male grows up thinking his mother is the Virgin Mary, and so naturally he thinks he is Jesus Christ, or God's gift to the world anyway, or to its women-folk at least.

Italian males find it very difficult to leave home. Their mothers make it hard for them to do so by making sure that their sons are so pampered and spoilt that they have no real wish to leave. Even when they are married, they continue to behave as if they aren't, taking their clothes home at least once a week for their mother to wash and iron.

It is quite normal for Italian males well over the age of thirty to be living in the parental home, behaving just like teenagers in northern European countries. Why give up a life of luxury and financial security with a woman who treats you as the Son of God for an uncertain future with a woman who might ask you do things in the home that you have never learnt to do, like making your bed or drying the dishes?

La mamma

Italian women are brilliant actresses. Although they are completely emancipated and behave exactly as they want, when and where they want, they go through life pretending that they are quiet and subservient and that Italian men rule the roost.

It is really only an act, for Italian women rule the family. Italian girlfriends and wives know that image is important to their men, so they let them think they are big, macho, decision-makers. However, they also know that their menfolk have been so spoilt as children that they are more or less incapable of competing effectively on the great stage of life, and are able to do very little for themselves apart from looking good, drinking coffee, fathering children, and then playing with the children's toys. Italian women know all this because they have always taken great care to spoil their male children, thereby rendering them almost completely dependent. The secret of power is handed on by one generation of Italian women to the next: faking subservience is a small price to pay for power in the family.

I bambini

Italian children are allowed to be both seen and heard; in fact, they must be both seen and heard, and be on show all the time, except, of course, between 2 and 5 p.m., when they should be having their afternoon nap. All Italian children take a siesta, which means they are not too tired to take part in the *passeggiata*, when all over Italy people begin moving into the empty streets, to see and be seen, after the sun has begun to lose its heat. Many Italians never lose the habit of taking an afternoon nap, which explains why they and their children still seem to have boundless energy at midnight.

Children are often dressed as miniature adults and exposed to most aspects of adult life. They are welcomed at restaurants and expected to be present at all family activities and functions. They grow up much faster than their northern European peers and learn the key skills necessary for performing on the great stage of life at an early age. Italians are on the whole wonderful with children, even with obstreperous and ugly ones. As the old Neapolitan saying runs, *Ogni scarafone è bello a mamma soja* ('Every beetle is beautiful to its mother').

I nonni

Generally wielding the financial power and patronage within the family, the *nonni* (grandparents) are careful to spoil their grandchildren and inculcate in them the importance of returning favours for presents, thereby ensuring that when they, in turn, become *nonni,* their families will look after them well.

Belonging to an Italian family is a cradle to the grave contractual agreement.

Gli animali

For the Italians animals must have a practical use. Dogs must be able to bark at strangers and so be justified as guard dogs. Cats must be able to keep the mice at bay. Pets must amuse the children or perform a role as a fashion accessory. If animals fit none of these categories then they can only serve one purpose, they must be for eating.

The Italians will kill and eat almost anything that runs, flies or swims. When the shooting season starts in

September, the Italian male will dress up as a hunter, go to the countryside and blast away at everything that moves. Then he will return home triumphant in the evening with three dead skylarks and two dead hedge-hogs. These will be served up to the family with enormous pride at lunch the next day – at last *il papà* has done something useful for the family.

L'amicizia

The importance of friendship may be over-shadowed by the role of the family, but it plays a key role in Italian society. Italians are highly gregarious people and love belonging to groups or cliques. The idea of belonging to a group is seen as natural and essential.

'Real' friendships are usually formed early on in life, at school or with neighbours, and tend to be lifelong and important. Groups of old friends are often comparatively closed and admit few new members.

Other 'real' friends can be made at university, at work, playing sport, and so on, but tend to be more rare. These friendships should perhaps be considered 'useful' rather than 'real'. Most adult Italians belong to a whole network of 'useful' friendships: the good dentist who will extract your teeth 'at half-price', the smart lawyer who will present your case free of charge, the lady in the bread shop who will always keep a loaf of your favourite bread.

Then there are 'dangerous' friendships – those you would be better off without, often linked to 'offers you can't refuse'. The sister of one of Italy's most famous judges, who was killed by a car bomb while leading the Palermo courts in their fight against the mafia, is continuing her brother's fight. She says she has few friends, commenting that it is exactly when people start being too friendly that you really have to worry about your life.

Visitors sometimes accuse the Italians of wearing their hearts on their sleeves, but this 'superficial' friendliness is often misunderstood. They are being treated as friends without anything but friendship being expected in return, something that Italians rarely grant each other. There are no strings attached: they will not be asked to help Salvatore's second cousin Concetta find a job when she comes to their country in the spring.

La casa

The Italians are eminently practical, and everything must have its use. Italian homes tend to be small and beautifully looked after, with the number of rooms kept to a minimum. Guest bedrooms are rare – "They can stay in a hotel, can't they?" Much of Italian life is lived in public, and so the home tends to be treated like a star's dressing room where Italians go to change and relax between acts. Most homes have one room where visitors can be welcomed which contains all the best furniture and pictures. However, this is usually off-limits to the family and so rarely used that in winter it is freezing cold; there seems no sense in heating it.

Many Italian families have a second or even third home, at the seaside or in the mountains. These are generally small, one- or two-room apartments with bunk beds where the whole family can sleep on holiday.

Land tends to be considered much too valuable for growing flowers (unless, of course, they can be sold), so Italian gardens are almost always kitchen gardens, and the Italians are brilliant at growing large quantities of wonderful fruit and vegetables on tiny plots of land, or even on their balconies.

Obsessions

Outsmarting Other Italians

The concept of outsmarting other Italians, who can then be mocked as slow and gullible (or *fesso*), is central to the Italian psyche, and is generally regarded as a positive virtue, as long as it is successful. Thus Italians tend to rather admire and even envy the clever dick (*il furbo*) who connives to get to the front of the traffic jam and then jumps the red light and goes roaring off ahead of everyone else.

If he is seen by the traffic police, chased and stopped, the *furbo* will then swear blind that his wife is about to give birth, and that he has to get home as fast as possible to get her to the maternity hospital, and go roaring off again, with a police escort. Anything goes in the pursuit of outsmarting others, from the bending of rules whenever possible, to the telling of lies. Italians grow up knowing that they have to be economical with the truth. All other Italians are, so if they didn't play the game they would be at a serious disadvantage. They have to fabricate to keep one step ahead.

Not getting away with something is the main risk involved, but it is generally regarded as an acceptable one. After all, that ticket for shooting the lights might never need to be paid, especially if the driver's cousin who works in the police department reminds the traffic policeman that they both support the same football team and lets him know that the driver just happens to have a spare ticket for the big match on Sunday afternoon.

Losing face is considered far worse than being found out, and Italians will often make and accept a whole series of what seem to be completely unnecessary or highly improbable excuses in order not to be seen to be at fault.

Convenient euphemisms like, "I mislaid your phone number" or "Your letter never arrived", are so much easier to say than admitting that you underestimated the importance of a swift reply, and thus appearing a complete *fesso*.

Avoiding Tax

Italy has the greatest number of taxes and some of the highest rates of taxation in Europe. This may look unfair, but as it is also the country where the people are famous for not paying their taxes, the government has always to take this factor into consideration when calculating their demands. This has led to some misunderstandings. When Trieste passed from the Austro-Hungarian Empire to Italy in 1918, the people paid the taxes they were asked to pay. The tax inspectors immediately asked them to pay double the next year, working on the principle that people never paid more than 50% of what they could pay.

By and large salaried workers are unable to avoid paying taxes as these are deducted at source. Recent statistics reveal that salaried workers make up 70% of the workforce but pay 85% of all taxes levied on earnings.

Servicing the Italian national debt is no easy job, and the Government often has recourse to financial amnesties to bring in revenue; for example, the building amnesty of 1994 permitted all those who had broken the laws relating to construction to regularise their position by paying a fine.

These amnesties are quite successful in raising money, but the reverse side is that they tend to encourage others to risk breaking the law, and so the cycle continues. They also help to explain the building speculation, often executed with an almost total absence of planning permission, which has ruined some of Italy's most beautiful beaches.

It has been estimated that up to a third of Italy's economic activity is carried out unofficially and so is outside the reach of the official statistics and thus, by implication, of the tax office. This *economia sommersa* (hidden economy) is made up of *lavoro nero* (black-work, i.e. moonlighting) at all levels (not only the plumber, but the surgeon, too, will work *in nero* whenever possible) and of income from criminal activities (drug smuggling, cigarette smuggling, prostitution, bribes). It explains why Italians manage to look so affluent, while their country is always on the verge of bankruptcy.

Security – The Key Factor

Italians are obsessed with security. Given the high level of crime (in Turin, a car theft every 57 minutes, a bag snatching every 86 minutes and a burglary every 2 hours), they have to be. So they produce wonderful alarm systems and padlocks, turning their houses and shops into miniature fortresses.

Yet there are often weak points. Incredibly well-secured doors will only be held in place by the flimsiest hinges, and that car alarm, which is so sensitive even a light shower of rain will set it off, may never be switched on.

L'amore

Love is taken very seriously by Italians – 99% of all their songs are about love – and it is endlessly thought about and debated, for after all, what is life without *amore*?

The debate covers a large number of key issues: What effect does falling in love have on your diet? Is love good for your health? Is love possible without sex? Is sex possible without love? Is universal love possible? And what about free love? The debate has endless scope and involves the entire nation. Whole television series are devoted to couples in love, couples out of love, couples looking for love, children and love, elderly people and love, and so on. While no-one knows how much time Italians spend actually making love, they spend a great deal of their time talking and thinking about it.

Italian men are expected to behave in a certain way. The very popular ex-President, Sandro Pertini, was a happily married man whose private and public morality nobody would have dreamt of criticising. When, in his mid-seventies, he was admiring the latest Alfa Romeo sports car and was heard to say: "What a beautiful car! Not for one's wife, of course", he was just being very Italian.

Whether or not Latins really are dynamic lovers, Italians bask in the glory achieved by their forebears and millions of people continue to think that they are. However, it seems that trying to live up to their reputation causes widespread problems of premature ejaculation and even failure to perform. In March 1993 the national newspaper, *La Stampa,* printed a long article on a survey by the Italian Institute of Sexologists which stated that two million male Italians suffer from impotence. Unfortunately, all it could suggest as the most effective solution to solving their problem was to listen to music.

Most verbal insults are related to the sexual behaviour of men and women. Men will accuse women of free and easy sexual morals, calling them *puttana* (whore) and so on, and though women rarely swear, when they do, they tend to attack the virility of men by calling them gay, old, or impotent.

Nevertheless, the legend of the Latin Lover lives on, and Italian males can read other articles in the newspapers with greater satisfaction, like the one reporting the comforting fact that Italian condoms are half a centimetre longer than those used in other countries.

Il tradimento

Love is linked to another national obsession, *il tradimento,* betrayal. Betrayal, or rather fear of betrayal, is what keeps relationships passionate in Italy, and what is love without passion?

Magazines such as Italian *Cosmopolitan* regularly reveal that large numbers of Italian husbands betray their wives, and vice versa. Despite this, betrayal is still a dangerous game in Italy: enraged fathers, brothers, uncles and cousins will not think twice before resorting to violence to defend the honour of the family. Italians are famous for *la vendetta,* and many a *faida* (blood feud) is begun which can continue for generations, or at least until the original cause has long since been forgotten.

Leisure and Pleasure

The Italians live life to the full, and do not feel in the least bit guilty leading a life of leisure and pleasure twenty-four hours a day, seven days a week, fifty-two weeks a year. This is what life is all about: Italians do not live to work, they work to live.

Lo sport

Football is far and away the most important sport in Italy. Matches are played on Sunday afternoons and Italian men are often to be seen holding radios to their ears as they take their family out for a Sunday afternoon stroll. When the national team is playing in the World Cup, the whole nation comes to a halt and everybody forgets their regional differences – in front of the television.

The only other sport taken seriously at a national level is cycling, and the progress of the Italian competitors in the *Giro d'Italia* and the *Tour de France* is followed with rapt attention.

The Italians are not brought up with physical education classes – few Italian schools have good sports facilities – and it is hard to find anyone participating seriously in sport (beautifully-dressed Italian joggers are easily overtaken by the average walker as they flaunt their way around the park on a Sunday morning). Despite this, Italy regularly manages to produce world and Olympic champions in a whole variety of sports, from swimming and fencing to rowing and shooting, with both the competitors and their country relishing and making the most of every opportunity for occupying the centre stage.

Lo shopping

Italians love shopping. Their cities are full of wonderful craftsmen and skilled tailors, as well as shops catering for every taste and whim. The sheer quality and luxury of the goods on display in the main streets is stunning. As are the price tags. But although only the rich and famous will actually enter Gucci, Armani and Valentino shops and buy, the Italians are not put off, for they know that the end price of the goods on display could turn out be very different, especially when sooner or later they may turn up in the sales or in a street market.

Shopping is considered fun, especially at the markets where there are real bargains to be found, but you should never inquire too deeply into the provenance of the goods. As long as it fits, does it really matter that the beautiful little black Moschino cocktail dress which is being offered to you at 50,000 lira is the same as the one you saw on sale in the Via Veneto last night at 500,000? Of course, the risk is yours, and that real bargain could just as easily be a real fake.

Italians have no false pride with regard to trade. Haggling is acceptable in the markets, and customers are expected to ask for a discount in shops. Italians will also sell you, or each other, anything and everything, from their grandmother to their next-door neighbour, at the right price, of course. In Naples, for example, the street kids will unscrew your car number plate at one set of traffic lights and sell it back to you at the next, with a smile and, naturally, at a bargain price.

Sense of Humour

Italians have a good sense of humour and are able to laugh at themselves as well as at others. But as they also have great respect for the role they are playing, they prefer not to ruin the effect with levity. They are very conscious of public dignity, and when playing an institutional part, will act it with great formality and aplomb. The law professor will not lard his lectures with wisecracks. This attitude often means that Italian academic papers and conferences are among the most serious and therefore perhaps most boring in the world. There may be an occasional vein of discreetly veiled irony in the comments and presentation, but you have to listen hard for it.

Because the crime of *vilipendio* – which makes those who insult politicians or public officials in writing liable to prosecution on criminal charges – does not include drawn illustrations, Italian newspapers have developed political cartoons to a fine art. Cartoonists satirise political figures and situations with devastating irony.

Italy's most famous political cartoonist of the day is Forattini whose portrayals of the quirks and idiosyncrasies of leading political figures on the front page of *La Repubblica* have made him an important national figure. Few Italians realised the power of the Socialist Party leader Bettino Craxi until Forattini started drawing pictures of him dressed up as a certain Benito...

Italians enjoy seeing themselves through another's eyes. They get a further running commentary in the press from Italian cartoonist, Altan, whose pithy observations on their character are sent from his comfortable perch in Brazil. Here are two examples:

> Two builders wearing their origami hats (builders in Italy will fold a newspaper page into the shape of a boat, and wear it as a sunhat) are sitting on a pile of bricks having their lunch. One is reading an old newspaper: "It says here that the Italians are a bunch of individualists." "Who cares?" says the other. "That's their business."

> A conversation between two young women, reflecting on the antics of their lovers: "One has to admit that Italian men are extraordinary," says one. "Definitely, says the other, "I only wish they were normal."

The Italians' obsession with keeping an eye on their neighbours is reflected by their humour, which has few jokes about other nationalities, but lots about other Italians. For example, the people from Genoa are generally regarded as being stingier than the Scots:

Having decided to hang a picture in the living room, a Genoese father says to his son "Go and ask the neighbours if we can borrow their hammer". The boy returns empty-handed: "They say they're sorry but they can't find it." "Bloody mean of them," says the father. "OK, go and get ours, then."

La Cultura

Italians have enormous respect for culture. They know the value of their national heritage and that it is one of the main sources of their country's wealth.

Money is, and always has been, a driving force behind Italian creative art, but it is not the only one. Religion, a sense of beauty, and a gift for understanding the spirit of place are also important. Perhaps the most important of all is the Italian's innate pride in making things beautiful – *fatta ad arte*. Things don't necessarily have to work well, they don't necessarily have to last, but they have to look good. And if they are beautiful, the Italians will make the effort to make them work well and to make them last.

This is the link between a dress by Valentino, a car by Pininfarina, a glass gondola blown in a small workshop on one of the islands in the Venetian lagoon, a roadside madonna and child, and a plate of fresh pasta.

Italian prisoners of war on the Orkney Islands during World War II were given a Nissen hut to use as their chapel. They carefully decorated the inside, painting it with baroque trompe l'oeil and turning it into a work of art. Fifty years later, ex-prisoners regularly return to make sure their chapel is still beautiful.

Melodrama

Italian life is, and always has been, melodramatic, which helps explain the popularity of operas of the 19th century and soap operas of today. Plumbers can be heard singing well-known arias while they work, and cleaning ladies save their pennies for a ticket to dress up to the nines and attend La Scala.

Karaoke has enjoyed an incredible boom in Italy, giving ordinary Italians a wonderful opportunity to satisfy their narcissism by being 'on show'. What could be more fun than singing your heart out in front of your friends and family?

Television

If the Italians didn't actually invent trash television, they have certainly developed it to a fine art. Even on the three national channels there is a lack of finesse that would be considered extremely slapdash anywhere else. Viewers are often treated to completely blank screens, and programmes regularly start several minutes later than scheduled. Newscasters are frequently caught reading items that have no relation to what is happening on the screen.

Italian viewing is mainly made up of films, cartoons and soap operas, which have been imported and dubbed.

The dubbing can be appalling: in the love scene from *A Fish called Wanda*, even John Cleese's utterances in Russian, which were supposed to excite Jamie Lee Curtis to a frenzy, were rendered into Italian.

On the other hand, the astonishing success of second-rate American soap operas in Italy is largely due to the real passion of the Italian versions, where the dubbing has served to cover up the poor quality of the original dialogue. The Italian version of *The Beautiful and the Bold* resulted in its little-known American stars achieving cult status in Italy and being better known than the members of the government.

Most home-grown productions are variety shows which cater for so-called 'family viewing' and as Italian children are usually still up and about at 10.30 p.m., they tend to go on interminably all evening, offering the same basic ingredients of quizzes, games and competitions interspersed with song and dance routines and advertisements.

The alternatives for family viewing are dubbed Walt Disney imports and wildlife documentaries, or 'Euro' programmes like *It's a Knockout* and *The Eurovision Song Contest* which have little success in the rest of Europe, but in Italy dominate the audience share.

Other programmes take their cue from *Candid Camera* and give viewers the chance to see unwitting participants reduced to tears and rage without knowing they are being watched by an audience of millions. In *Complotto di Famiglia* (Family Conspiracy) for instance, Maria accompanies her husband to an important business dinner for the first time. As the evening progresses, it becomes increasingly clear that the glamorous hostess in a tight pink suit is paying too much attention to Maria's husband. At a certain point she asks Maria to 'lend her husband to her for a bit'. The husband seems to acquiesce.

The ensuing scene is fraught with anguish and emotion, but the programme ends before viewers can see whether or not Maria and her husband manage to save their marriage.

Late-night viewing is for adults only, and 'high quality' films compete with programmes like *Colpo Grosso* (Jackpot) where participants can strip to win bonus prizes.

The one bright spark in the entire canon is a programme called *Blob*, which devotes an hour each evening to showing (without commentary) a cunningly-edited collection of the previous day's televised news and events. Presented in this way it gives the Italians a daily dose of two things they enjoy most in life, laughing at others' mistakes and debunking their politicians.

The Press

Italian newspapers are expensive and have a limited readership. The average daily circulation in 1994 was under 6.5 million although the actual number of readers is difficult to calculate since many Italians read newspapers available in public places, in the library, the town square, or the bar, and others buy more than one newspaper a day.

Most Italian newspapers are serious local papers with a national bent. Others are closely linked to political parties, like *Il Giornale* to Silvio Berlusconi's Forza Italia and *L'Unità* to the Democratic Party of the Left. The daily newspaper with the widest circulation is the *Corriere dello Sport*, which publishes nothing but sporting news, reflecting perhaps the real interest of the Italian public.

For gossip the Italians buy and read glossy weekly magazines like *Oggi* (Today) and *Novella 2000*, where they can read all they want about the world of Hollywood and the British or Monégasque royal families. Despite Italy being the birthplace of the *paparazzi*, there are few juicy stories about the love lives and scandals of Italian politicians and people in high places, due to a long-standing tacit agreement between the powers that be and the Italian press.

Literature

Italy has a fine literary heritage. Famous writers from the past include Dante Alighieri, Boccaccio and Ariosto, while amongst the recent and current are Primo Levi, Italo Calvino, Alberto Moravia, Umberto Eco and Dario Fo. Their works tend to be looked on as 'great literature' and, as such, are usually reserved for studying at school, or appreciating on special occasions.

For more general reading, on trains or in bed, the Italians enjoy racy, international, best-selling block-busters by Harold Robbins and Wilbur Smith, or Judith Krantz and Danielle Steel.

Some literary genres are colour-coded. Yellow is used for thrillers and detective stories, black for the *cronaca nera* or crime pages in newspapers and magazines, and pink for romantic novelettes.

Perhaps the most successful literary genre in the country which gave the world that much-loved children's character, *Pinocchio*, is the comic. Italians adore book-length comics. They are often happiest of all reading the soft porn adventures of their imaginary heroes, like cowboy *Tex Willer*, sexy fashion victim *Valentina,* and the off-beat investigator of nightmares and inveterate womaniser, *Dylan Dog.*

The Eat-alian Way

The Italians are foodcentric people. Much of Italian life revolves around the growing, buying, preparing and, above all, eating of food. Whenever possible, meals are shared and eaten in company. The very word 'company' comes from two Italian words, *con* (with) and *pane* (bread), implying breaking bread in friendship.

But the Italian meal in company is much more than breaking bread, for Italian enthusiasm knows no bounds when it comes to organising a meal. First there must be the *antipasti* (starters), usually a minimum of five, then the first course (the *primo)*, with a choice of different pasta or rice dishes; next the main course (the *secondo)*, which will be meat or fish with the accompanying vegetables (the *contorno)*; then cheese, and finally the dessert (the *dolce)* followed by coffee (*espresso)*. The meal can happily take from two to five hours to consume. If it was lunch, you have a couple of hours to recover before suppertime.

Food

The Italians have always appreciated quality and keep the very best of foods for themselves. Italy is still an agricultural nation and its small farmers (*i contadini*), who wield enormous power in the community, are highly practical men. They pay little attention to EU directives and farm according to time-honoured ways, harvesting wonderful produce.

Many city-dwellers have relatives in the countryside who will keep them stocked up with home-grown and home-produced specialities. The salad and wine that are put on the table in honour of a guest will be very special, and every bite and drop will be truly memorable.

The Italians acknowledge the changing of the seasons and the different delicacies linked to each. The whole family will take part in preparing the *passata di pomodoro* (tomato purée) in the late summer, go mush-rooming in September, grape-picking in October, and in March collect those exquisite young dandelion leaves that add a zest to salads.

The secret behind Italian cooking lies not only in the fact that the ingredients are fresh and of good quality, but also that most Italians, male and female, are excellent cooks. They learn how to cook when young, and a look at Italian cookbooks shows that the writers start from the premise that their readers already know how. Italian recipes are much less precise than British or American ones and don't say, 'carefully add 150 grams of this' or 'slowly pour in 4 fluid ounces of that'; they simply say, 'take a pinch of this', or 'add a couple of drops of that'.

Despite their admiration for many things American, the Italians have been remarkably resistant to some American foodways. Coca-Cola and hamburgers have been accepted, but peanut butter and baked beans have not; breakfast cereals are advertised, but without much success. Italy is the only country in the world where the marketing strate-gies of McDonald's have been hampered by the birth of the Slow Food Movement.

Grain, Grape and Grappa

Italians are the world's largest consumers of whisky, especially malt – an average bar in Italy will stock a greater selection than most pubs in Scotland – and beer is becoming fashionable with the young, especially if it is strong and imported. But what really runs in the nation's veins is wine.

Italian wines range from purple-black table wines frothing in your glass to sparkling dry whites. They are generally drunk locally and young, and the fact that many of the best Italian wines are unknown outside Italy serves to keep their prices reasonable. Country wines vary from the regal to the robust, each with its own distinct character. As a village salami-maker remarked as he savoured a glass of his region's *vino nero*: "A wine is like a man; it can have flaws and still be pleasing."

On the whole, Italians drink only when they eat, but this does not mean that they stint themselves. The meal will be preceded by an *aperitivo*, and each course will be accompanied by a different wine, with a sparkling wine reserved for the dessert.

Unfortunately, the human stomach was not designed for such conspicuous over-indulgence, so the Italians have thought up a variety of ingenious ways to help the digestive system cope. They drink mineral waters throughout the meal, and after it can choose from a host of evil-tasting medicinal preparations called *digestivi*, or perhaps a fiery *grappa*, in the hope that it will spur their jaded innards into action.

Despite these precautionary measures, the hard work that Italian digestive systems are asked to perform often leads to their going on strike, and constipation is a common complaint. Other nations' remedies are suspect, and Italians refuse to eat the German-style wholemeal breads and American-style high fibre cereals which might solve their problems, in much the same way as they refuse to change their eating habits, by eating, for example, a little less.

Health

The most common Italian illness is hypochondria. Italians are in general extremely healthy people who spend a great deal of their time thinking that they should feel healthier than they do. This is partly because they imagine that everyone else feels better than they do, and partly because they have absurd expectations about their own health. They worry constantly about it. Could that stomach ache be the beginnings of stomach cancer? (forgetting that they ate too much the night before). Might that headache be the beginnings of a brain tumour? (forgetting that they drank too much the night before).

Italians are happy to spend vast sums of money servicing their hypochondria. If their doctor tells them they are in the pink of health, they will go to a private specialist. If this specialist finds nothing wrong, they will go to another one, and so on, until they find a doctor who is prepared to prescribe. The prescription will then be taken to the local chemist and discussed at length, before the medicine is bought (and one or two others that the chemist has recommended as well; after all, you never know...). Consequently, the typical Italian bathroom cupboard is crammed with as many medicines as most dispensaries, most of them years beyond their expiry date.

Problems can occur when Italians are genuinely ill. They have already exhausted their doctor's patience and precious time, and they have already visited half the specialists in town. One possible solution is the hospital Casualty Department. But is that ingrowing toenail a serious enough ailment? Or might the hospital surgeon remove the wrong toenail in his zeal?

Italian news reports are full of hospital horror stories, like the one about the Franciscan friar who went into hospital for a hernia operation and came out with only half his trachea. Or the footballer who had the wrong knee operated on. Despite the fact that there is little real evidence of Italian hospitals being any better or worse than those of other European countries, Italians will often travel to Switzerland or France for treatment, in the unshakeable belief that hospitals function better elsewhere.

Dental Care

Most Italians look wonderfully fit and healthy, until they open their mouths. Dental treatment in Italy is very expensive and, unfortunately for them but fortunately for their dentists, Italians tend to wait until they have serious problems with their teeth before making an appointment.

They treat their teeth as they do their ancient monuments, waiting until they are almost beyond repair rather than investing in continuous maintenance. Why bother to do a (temporary) fixing when you could wait until there is a really big job to be done?

Custom and Tradition

The Italians traditionally celebrate Christmas at home with the family and Easter with friends, '*Natale con i tuoi, Pasqua con chi vuoi*' (Christmas with your own, Easter with whomever you want). But Easter Monday (called *Pasquetta*, little Easter) is always spent on a big family picnic. Never mind that it often rains on Easter Monday (the weather having changed with the Easter moon), this picnic is never called off.

Every Italian town and village celebrates its own saint's day. Milan takes the day off for St. Ambrose, Turin for

St. John, Naples for St. Gennaro and Rome for St. Peter.

Most places also have a *sagra* or festival week devoted to a composer, or food, or a sports event, or an award named after some local poet or politician. These can be on the grand scale, like the great *palio* (horse race) at Siena, but often they are local affairs, where the people take time off to do what Italians enjoy most, eating good food and drinking good wine at a leisurely pace in good company.

Annual holidays in Italy are mostly taken in August, when the factories in the great northern cities close as the heat of the summer makes city life unbearable, and most families head for the mountains or the seaside to cool down. Life becomes difficult for those who stay behind, as the shops close too, and it isn't always easy to find the basic necessities of life, while those on holiday do their best to recreate the hustle and bustle of city life on the beach.

Other important holidays in Italy include 8th March, when women exchange yellow mimosa and celebrate their pride in being women, 1st May, when half the country is involved in Don Camillo-style first communions and the other half in Peppone-style workers' parades, and 1st November, when most Italians take part in serious ancestor worship, visiting their dead in the cemeteries where they repose in multi-decker tombs, stacked one above the other, like so many filing cabinets.

The days before the abstinence of Lent begins on Ash Wednesday are dedicated to celebrating Carnival (from the Latin *carnem levare* – literally 'put away meat'), with fancy dress parades and parties climaxing in the Shrove Tuesday (*Martedì Grasso*) festivities, the biggest of which take place in Venice and Viareggio. The Italian Carnival dates back to the pagan Roman feasts of Saturnalia and Lupercalia. For some, Carnival is a time for dressing up as Harlequin or Pulcinella, or dressing up their children and taking them to the parade and the funfair; for others it is a wonderful excuse for behaving outrageously.

Privilege

Many Italians have special *privilegi* or belong to privileged groups or areas where they pay few taxes, or don't have to pay taxes at all. Semi-autonomous regions, like the Aosta Valley, are comparatively happy to remain Italian as long as they continue to receive vast subsidies from central government, only paying, for example, a quarter of the price the rest of Italy pays for petrol.

Italian Members of Parliament and Members of the European Parliament are amongst the highest paid in Europe and also receive preferential treatment wherever they go. The same privilege is given to all those in positions of power and authority, from the members of the local council to the local chief of police. *Le autorità* (local dignitaries) can count on the fact that for anything that really matters – important football matches or concerts – they have a permanent reservation of the best seats.

The Catholic Church

The Italians like to think that Italy is a Catholic country, even if they are highly irreverent towards their clergy and pay little more than lip service to papal diktats, such as those concerning birth control: despite the Vatican's line, Italy has the lowest birth rate in Europe, with an average of 1.3 children per family. (Unless the trend is reversed, the population of Italy will have shrunk by some 300,000 by the year 2008.)

By and large, papal and episcopal encyclicals are ignored, as religion is preferred to be visual and tangible: pictures of the Madonna, *il Papa* (the Pope), local saints and football stars are pasted everywhere – in public places, private homes, and even on personal computers.

The Pope is Italy's only crowned Head of State and, because of his position, his visits to Italian cities are treated with much greater interest and excitement than those of the President or the Prime Minister. He is the only leader in Italy who can fill a stadium with his fans, and the only visitor *le autorità* will make an effort to impress, painting the stadium walls white on the morning of his visit, so that no offensive graffiti will offend his holy eyes.

Superstition

The Italians worry about objects, events, behaviour and (especially) people who they think cause, or might cause, them misfortune. Many protect themselves, their cars and their houses with an array of prayers and amulets (some of them Christian and others definitely not), and spend great sums of money visiting a whole series of astrologers, witches and charlatans, as a kind of insurance policy against 'the evil eye'.

They also make good practical use of their superstitions. An Italian had a dream that he was sitting with Pope John XXIII listening to an old 33 r.p.m. record. When he woke up he told the dream to his neighbour. Her first reaction was: "23 and 33. I'll play those numbers on the Lotto (state bingo) tomorrow."

Many people watch the cycle of the moon carefully, not just because of its effect on the human mind and body, but because of the effect it has on the sowing and harvesting of crops, and on the preservation of food and drink. Thus wine should always be bottled under the right moon; luckily it can be drunk under any moon.

Whether they are church-goers or not, Italians are fascinated by the unsolved mystery element of miracles. When an ordinary mass-produced statue of the Madonna started to cry tears of blood in a back-garden in Civitavecchia in spring 1995, the whole nation became involved in the debate ("Why did the bishop accept the miracle before the Vatican did?" "Why was the blood male?" and so on), and *le autorità* and tradespeople got ready to handle the armies of pilgrims who were expected in the city. In the event, common sense prevailed and only a handful of locals actually showed up at the scene.

However, this is the country with the most impressive reliquaries in Christendom; the country of Padre Pio; the country where the blood of San Gennaro in Naples has liquefied three times a year since August 1389. Never mind the fact that there are enough pieces of the True Cross around to build a basilica, or that St. Eulalia (the foster mother of Christ) must have had thirteen breasts, relics and miracles are good for keeping the faithful in the fold. Better still, they are good for business.

La Politica

Government

Centuries of government by foreign powers has given the Italians a strange idea of government. It is not viewed as a friendly public organism designed to protect and look after Italian interests at home and abroad. Rather it is seen as an alien, hostile organisation to which the people have no real link or sense of belonging, one which is hungry for taxes which will go into the pockets of the current group of fat cats that are running it. Fortunately, it can conveniently be blamed for the nation's problems.

An old political cartoon sums up the Italians' attitude to their government. A man is standing on his doorstep looking out at the pouring rain. The caption reads: 'It's raining. The Government's a bunch of crooks.'

Italy may look as if it has had an incredible number of different governments since the Second World War, but until 1994 its politics were basically dominated by one political party, the Christian Democrats, kept in power by a coalition of allies. *Cambio di governo* came to mean a cabinet reshuffle rather than a 'change of government'. So, as it was always obvious who would win any election, the majority of Italians became used to being on the winning side. Much of the present uncertainty in Italian politics is that people are no longer sure which is the winning side.

Politics

Italian politicians behave in much the same way as their ancestors. The power struggles, political corruption and clientalism that plagued the Late Roman Empire are alive and well in Italy today.

Italy is a country which seems to survive despite the efforts of its politicians to ruin it. The Italians love playing politics and the aim of the game is often difficult for foreigners to understand.

Achieving power and patronage are regarded as all-important goals; a Sicilian saying runs *Comandare è meglio di fottere* ('Ruling is better than screwing'). And yet, perversely, in Italian politics it is often considered more important to destroy what your rivals are trying to build than to try and build something yourself.

Unfortunately (or perhaps fortunately), the Italian people, like the Roman mob of old, can still be kept happy and quiet with 'bread and circuses' and Italian politicians and leaders know this. It is no accident that Italy has the best football league championship in the world. Matches starring the world's most expensive football players have replaced the gladiatorial combats and displays in the Colosseum. The Italians see nothing strange in this and carry on under the delusion that the rest of the world operates in exactly the same way, taking their cue from the old saying, *Tutto il mondo è paese* ('All the world's the same').

Left or Right

The labels of Italy's political parties have often been very confusing. The Liberals were never particularly liberal, the Socialists not especially socialist, the Communists definitely not communists, and the Christian Democrats neither very Christian nor very democratic.

Italians, particularly those on the left, worry enormously about what should be labelled right- and left-wing. Debates take place over whether karaoke is right-wing, or whether employing a home help is left-wing. These anxieties seems at last to be subsiding as people gradually realise that the vast majority of things cannot be classified as left-wing or right-wing and that really it makes little difference either way.

Referenda

From time to time the Italians are called upon to vote in referenda on important issues, such as divorce, abortion, nuclear power, the use of pesticides in farming and the number of television channels any one Italian citizen can own. This gives them a sense of being involved in political decision-making.

A referendum requires a 50% turn-out to be a valid quorum. Thus, despite an increasing number of Italians wishing to protect the country's ever-diminishing number of birds and beasts, a referendum on the issue only resulted in a 45% turn-out and new legislation was blocked. On the other hand, the Italians turned out in force to vote in favour of having television films and documentaries interrupted by commercials.

Bureaucracy

All Italians believe that long bureaucratic procedures are of the utmost importance, but for *gli altri*, of course, not for themselves. Without these procedures other Italians would most certainly get up to every kind of mischief. Moreover, there are so many powerful interests involved in the Italian bureaucratic system that it is unlikely that anything will change. For while the Italian state earns vast revenues from the fact that almost all bureaucratic or legal procedures involve *carta bollata* (taxable officially-stamped paper), the same procedures also keep hundreds of thousands of civil servants in gainful employment. The longer the bureaucratic process, the greater the number of people employed.

Furthermore, without the long bureaucratic process, there would be no point in circumventing it, and the thousands of *galoppini* (unofficial specialists in accelerating bureaucratic procedures) would also be without employment.

There are so many laws and ministerial directives in the Italian system (it has been calculated that to be entirely in line with the law, an Italian citizen should know some 800,000 rules), and they are so diverse, complicated and often contradictory, that their strict application can more or less paralyse any bureaucratic procedure. And because even minor civil servants have very strong powers in Italy, to accept, refuse or delay requests or procedures, they are treated with enormous respect and courtesy, especially when they are wearing uniform. Conversely, the officials 'become' their jobs when they are in uniform and expect to be treated with the kind of deference northern Europeans reserve for crowned Heads of State.

Italian bureaucracy needs to be approached tactically. If approached the wrong way, officials become intransigent and will make little or no effort to help you solve your problem. If approached the Italian way, it can be flexible enough to permit a solution to be found.

Every citizen knows that falling foul of the system, by upsetting the wrong official or not contacting the right *galoppino*, could mean years of waiting. Officials can make your life easy or difficult, depending upon their whims. A Californian teaching at an Italian university wanted to take some courses. In order to enrol he went to the university admissions office and was told that he would need a copy of his UCLA degree certificate, with a translation certified by the Italian consulate in Los Angeles. Having gone to California during the summer vacation and obtained the necessary certificate and translation, he returned to the admissions office. "Ah, very good, now all we need is a copy of your high school diploma." The Californian's protestations that obviously he couldn't have entered UCLA without a high school diploma were of no avail. According to the admissions office he had to return to Los Angeles, get it and have its translation certified by the Italian consulate there. In the end he was forced to do what he had wanted to avoid doing at the beginning, which was to ask one of his senior colleagues to do him a favour and intervene so that he could by-pass the official.

While officials are treated with respect by Italians, this is not the case for places or objects that are public. The Italian has no feeling that these things are his, and therefore he should treat them well. His house or flat will be spotlessly tidy and clean, but he will think nothing of leaving litter and rubbish untidily on the pavement and street outside; there they become the city council's responsibility, not his.

La mafia

Mafia is a word used all over the world both for criminal organisations and for coteries of power, so that people talk about a sports mafia, an arts mafia or a business mafia, yet the model is always the Italian mafia.

In Italy 'mafia' covers several different bodies each ruling over a well-defined territory, the main ones being the *Camorra* in the region around Naples, the *'Ndrangheta* in Calabria (the tip of the boot), and *Cosa nostra* in Sicily; but whatever its name, they mean the criminal organisation.

Mafia in all its local forms has for centuries been a way of life in the South of Italy – except for some for whom it has been a way of death. The reason for its success is simple enough: in the absence of a recognisable or effective government, it was the only organised system ordinary people could refer to when they needed say, a permit to work or to get married.

Most Italians are terrified and fascinated by the mafia at one and the same time. They know its tentacles of power reach to the highest levels in politics and business since the mafia have always specialised in making offers that cannot be refused, knowing that everything and everyone has their price. They also know that the code of *omertà* (silence) is so strong that the odds are that the mafia will never be defeated, and every time one of its tentacles is lopped off, hydra-like others will grow again, stronger than before.

The mafia is seen as a cancer that is slowly destroying the Italian state. The Italians have to live with it and alongside it, a state within a state, sharing their country with it as they always have done. And yet they secretly believe that, just as the right treatment in time might be able to cure a tumour, sooner or later the right treatment will be found and administered in time to defeat the mafia.

Much of the time the mafia is divided, as its various families fight out their latest power struggle in time-honoured ways. Dark-suited men carrying violin cases still burst into barbers' shops in the back streets of Palermo and gun down the bosses of rival clans. Luckily, the closest most Italians will ever get to the real thing is the latest gripping episode of the television series, now in its seventh sequel, *La Piovra* (The Octopus).

Business

Business in the private sector in Italy is dominated by a handful of families, such as Agnelli (cars), Pirelli (tyres), De Benedetti (computers), Berlusconi (TV channels) and Benetton (clothes). Although their companies are, in fact, vast conglomerates with a wide diversity of interests, they are run more like family businesses than multinational corporations. Power tends to be kept within the family group by a series of cross holdings. There is no similar concentration of power in any other western country.

The success of the Italian economy is also based on the skills, hard work and dynamism of the small and medium-sized companies in the North that produce a large part of the country's GNP. They are also mostly family-run businesses, organised in such a way as to minimise the payment of taxes and national insurance contributions. Italy is perhaps the only country in the world where employees appear to earn more than their employers, or so it would seem from their tax declarations. Similarly, professional people and craftsmen, like accountants, goldsmiths, dentists and lawyers, have few qualms about declaring subsistence level earnings while maintaining two or three houses, a race horse and three yachts.

The Italian Job

Every Italian mother dreams that her children, especially her male children, will achieve *lo starbene* – a state of well-being in their work. What this generally entails is finding a steady job and looking good behind a big desk in the air-conditioned office of a government department or government-owned bank or company. Though not particularly well-paid, these jobs entitle their holders to 13 or even 14 months' salary a year and offer all sort of perks including almost total job security and the possibility of retiring early on a full pension. Best of all, they are usually so undemanding that their holders can concentrate most of their energies on the family business, or on whatever really interests them: watching football, collecting stamps or just sitting, sipping coffee, reading comics.

Life in the average Italian office is like Italian life in general. Style and behaviour are important, and managerial and office staff should, of course, look and act the part. Punctuality has been taken a little more seriously since the advent of clocking in and out of work.

Office hours can be very long in the private sector (8.00 a.m. – 7.30 p.m. with only half an hour for lunch). However, things are very different in the public sector: some offices are only open to the public for two hours a week, and others are never open at all.

Many of the public holidays that Italians took for Saint's Days have now been surrendered, so the practice of *ponti* (building 'bridges' between the weekend and a national holiday) assumes greater importance. Holidays are planned long in advance so as to be able to link them to public holidays.

This is why Italian strikes usually take place on Mondays or Fridays. Strikes in Italy reveal Italian passion, patience and resourcefulness at its collective best. The *autostrada* and railways will be occupied, rubbish not collected and hunger strikes started – the nation will seem to be on the verge of chaos – and then an unexpected compromise will be reached when none seemed possible. Everyone will claim victory, no-one will be seen to lose face, and the situation will return to normal. Everybody will have enjoyed the strike.

Typically, when the La Scala orchestra went on strike on the opening night of the 1995 season, the conductor had a grand piano brought on stage and he and the soloists performed the whole concert without the orchestra, to rapturous applause.

Patronage

Patronage, or *raccomandazione*, along with its trading of favours, jobs and influence, is part and parcel of Italian business life. At its worst it is an evil that prevents things from growing in a healthy way; at its best it is a kind of old boy network that is necessary in a country where little, in terms, for example, of real qualifications, is quite what it seems.

In order to ensure fair play in the distribution of jobs in the public sector, and in an attempt to curb the problem of *raccomandazione*, the Italian authorities organise *concorsi* (job competitions), when jobs are advertised and then all the candidates are required to sit an exam to decide who are the most suitable for the job. When there are not too many candidates the system works reasonably well, but when 14,000 people applied to become dustmen in the region of Lombardy, the situation became more complicated. Undismayed, *le autorità* took over the local football stadium for the day and brought in desks and chairs from the schools.

Never mind the fact that the 'recommended' candidates will probably have been told the questions beforehand and that the great majority of candidates will be cheating as hard as they can, justice must not so much be done as be seen to be done.

Crime and Punishment

All Italians are individually perfect, but know that *gli altri* are imperfect. So Italian criminal law starts from the premise that you are guilty until you are proved innocent. Statistically, the chances of actually being caught in Italy are very low, and Italian criminals have few worries about the lives they lead.

Punishment tends to involve either fines or imprisonment or both. Although Italian prisons are generally overcrowded and not particularly pleasant places to spend time, they are more comfortable than those in northern Europe and the United States. Indeed, conditions for imprisoned mafia bosses are said to be very comfortable indeed, and are regularly criticised in public for being so.

Italians are brilliant conmen who always manage to find people ready to risk their all to make a quick buck. They are expert copiers and counterfeiters, and have long dominated the traffic in art works. The fact that there is no guarantee that the works are the real thing, and may well be stolen or faked by a craftsman, only adds to the spice of the trade. Whether the buyer is looking for a Roman vase or a Modigliani sculpture, the illegal Italian art world will find him what he wants.

Italian politicians have themselves set the example of corrupt behaviour by accepting vast bribes for fixing government contracts. The Italians chose to ignore this until the government of the day made the fatal mistake of muffing it – thus changing status in a flash from *furbo* to *fesso*.

The Police

There is a different police force for every occasion in Italy. There are national police, local police, traffic police, military police, financial police, railway police, secret police, private police, and so on.

The *carabinieri* are the most evident of Italy's police forces. As part of the army, they are often involved in military as well as police activities. Despite the fact that it is extremely difficult to join their ranks, and that their officers are supposed to be the best in the Italian army, they are not famed for their shining intellectual prowess. As a result, they are the butt of many Italian jokes, e.g:

In the middle of a lively conversation on a train, someone asked, "By the way, have you heard the latest joke about the *carabinieri*?" A gentleman sitting opposite visibly stiffened, saying, "Before you continue, I should perhaps point out that I am a retired General of the *Carabinieri*." "Don't worry, sir, we'll explain it to you later."

The Law

Italy's legal traditions are impressive and the country has a vast array of wonderful laws, to prevent any kind of injustice, inequality or corruption. On paper the Italian legal system, with its written civil and penal codes, seems more or less perfect.

The problems start with law enforcement. Italy's laws would be perfect without the Italians, who pay little attention to most of them. For example, although seatbelts are compulsory, few Italians actually wear them (in some parts of Italy there is even a roaring trade in T-shirts with seatbelts painted on them). The use of car horns is officially prohibited in built-up areas, where the maximum speed limit is 30 m.p.h., but these regulations are by and large completely ignored by both the public and the police, although the police will enforce them occasionally, especially when they see people driving cars with foreign or out-of-town number plates.

Because of the very serious difficulties the Italian government has in collecting taxes, a whole series of laws exist to make sure regulations are respected. For example, receipts issued by bars and restaurants as proof of payment should be carried a minimum of 50 metres before being thrown away.

Those who work in the Italian legal system are well-trained and fair. Judges have been given enormous powers in the hope of improving law enforcement, but judicial processes are often very slow. Ignorance of the law is no defence in the Italian system. It couldn't be, or offenders would never be brought to book.

Systems

Education

Compared with the educational systems of other countries, the Italians seem to have got theirs the wrong way round. The country of Maria Montessori, Italy's best schools are probably its pre-schools, after which things seem to gradually degenerate through elementary, middle and high schools into a chaotic university system.

Small children spend most of their day at school, but as they get older schooling becomes limited to mornings only. High schools are specialised and students study a variety of classical, scientific and technical subjects, depending on the specialisation they have chosen.

Admission to Italian universities is comparatively easy and, since few faculties restrict the number of students enrolling on courses, vast numbers enrol. The University of Rome, for example, has over 150,000 students on its books. As a result, courses are overcrowded and facilities inadequate. The fact that under a quarter of all those who matriculate in the universities actually graduate is perhaps a fair reflection of the inherent problems.

Many Italians are well-educated, despite the limitations of the system. They like the idea of studying and spend hours/weeks/months slaving over textbooks with highlighters in hand, learning the key sentences and concepts by heart. They are then tested in the oral exam, the *inter-*

rogazione, parroting all they have learned. Critical comment by students is not welcomed. A repetition of the teacher's or professor's own views and comments is regarded as the best approach – a hangover from the Counter-Reformation when the wrong answer might have led you to the stake.

There are no limits to the number of times students can take exams, and some will refuse to accept a mark they don't consider good enough. As the only limitation to staying at the university is the payment of annual fees, many students continue studying well into middle age.

Examinations are mostly oral (perhaps because cheating is so rife in written exams). Italians fear that the other candidates in an exam will cheat and so they will cheat too. Cheating is considered more or less acceptable, but being caught cheating is not.

Transport

Italy's public transport system is generally quick and efficient, in spite of the country's difficult terrain and crowded cities. The Italian autostradas and rail network are among the most impressive feats of engineering in Europe, passing under mountains and over river valleys to link the various parts of Italy.

Trains usually run to schedule, despite the absence of an authoritarian government. One of Mussolini's more successful moves, and perhaps the only one he is universally remembered for, was persuading people that his government improved the efficiency of public transport; research has since proved that it made little or no impact on it at all, with trains being just as punctual in the periods before and during his regime as after it.

La Lingua

Until the end of the Second World War Italian was not widely spoken. It was essentially a written language, used by administrators and bureaucrats and a small caste of academics and the then members of the ruling class.

The advent of television in Italy was a prime force in spreading Italian. Now almost all Italians understand Italian and most young Italians speak it.

One of the many beauties of the Italian language is the ease with which dimension, value or meaning can be altered by simply changing in countless ways the ending of nouns and adjectives. Thus, a shoe (*scarpa*) can become Cinderella's slipper (*scarpina*) or a skiing/hiking boot (*scarpone*); but doing a *scarpetta* ('filling a little shoe') means dunking a bit of croissant in one's coffee.

A love (*amore*) can become a sweetheart (*amoroso*), or a cupid (*amorino*), or a mistress (*amante*). Italian men who hear of a *bella donna*, a beautiful woman, will wonder if she is in fact *bellissima* (stunning) or just *bellina* (quite pretty); maybe she is a *bellona* (well past her prime, but still a poser) or perhaps she is *belloccia* (passable, in all senses of the word). And is she an imposing *donnona* or a diminutive *donnina*? Is she worth very little (*donnetta*) or will she charge a fee (*donnaccia*)? The only way for the Latin lover to find out is by having a go, unless he is a *donnicciola* – one who is too timorous to try.

Italian has bequeathed to the world a vast number of musical terms: *pianoforte, sonata, aria, primadonna, concerto, adagio, pizzicato, pianissimo, soprano, maestro, virtuoso* and *castrato*. And restaurants world-wide offer *pasta, pizza, mozzarella, zabaglione, grissini, cappuccino, amaretto* and *sambuca*.

For their part, the Italians have adopted and adapted English/American words with huge enthusiasm – *lifting* (face-lift), *telemarketing, cliccare sul mouse* (to click on the mouse), *lo zapping* (to change channels). They also use English words that English-speakers would hardly recognise: *'Dribbling'*, is the title of a Sunday night television feature which presents the highlights of the day's football matches. It regularly includes interviews with Italian football stars, who invariably refer to their trainers as *'il Mister'*. They even invent English words, which they then proceed to export, sometimes with surprising success, for example, *body,* which threatens to replace *leotard.*

Dialects

But when they are at home in their villages Italians speak the local dialects or languages, which can be almost impossible for *gli altri* in other regions to understand. In 1992, the European Parliament found that of the EU's 28 minority language communities, 13 were in Italy. There are French-speaking Italians in the Aosta Valley, German-speaking Italians in the Alto Adige, Slovene- and Serbo-Croat-speaking Italians in Trieste, and Albanian- and Greek-speaking Italians in Puglia, while in Sardinia there are Catalan-speaking Italians.

Most regions also have their own local dialect that is both structurally and lexically very different from Italian. 60% of Italians speak a dialect and 14% no other language than their dialect. A man from the southern region of Puglia, who has lived in Piedmont for twenty years, has a Piedmontese neighbour who greets him every day as he leaves for work. The Pugliese man speaks Italian, and the Piedmontese man understands him. But, because the Piedmontese man doesn't speak Italian and the Pugliese has never bothered to learn Piedmontese, their conversation forever remains one-sided.

The Author

Brought up in England, Martin Solly first became enamoured of Italy as a student, staying with his *amici* in a superb farmhouse complete with swimming pool. The red-earthed landscapes of Tuscany, Renaissance culture, Chianti and mouthwatering *tortellini* and *zucchini* convinced him that the Italians enjoyed the ultimate in sybaritic living.

After working on farms, and in bars, restaurants, bookstores and schools, he settled in Piedmont with the intention of improving his knowledge of things Italian.

He little realised this would include a beautiful Piedmontese girl, and ignoring the old Italian saying *Moglie e buoi dei paesi tuoi* ('Choose your wife and your cattle from your own back-yard') he married her. They now live happily with their two Anglo-Italian daughters in Turin.

The author of a dozen books on English language and literature, Martin Solly teaches at Turin University, refusing even in the coldest weather to wear a vest. He does however, drive an Alfa-Romeo.